CRITICAL THINKING: GRA
TABLE OF CONTENTS

MW00963686

TEACHER INTRODUCTION

Overview

Steck-Vaughn Critical Thinking is a program designed to teach thinking skills. The skills are organized according to Benjamin Bloom's *Taxonomy of Educational Objectives.** These skills include some of the seven intelligences from the theory of multiple intelligences, such as linguistic, spatial, and logical-mathematical. Pupils are taught skills that have been identified as being particularly helpful in developing four stages of thinking - Knowledge, Comprehension, Application, and Analysis.

Program Philosophy

Direct teaching of thinking skills provides pupils with the opportunity to focus on **thinking** rather than on specific content. Practicing these skills will enable students to develop strategies which will enhance their ability to do well not only on standardized tests, but also in real-life situations.

Pupils who have had the opportunity to practice skills are better able to transfer them to other areas of the curriculum. *Steck-Vaughn Critical Thinking* contains practice pages for every skill presented in the program. Pupils need to know whether or not they are on the right track when they are practicing a new skill. Without feedback, a pupil might continue to practice a skill incorrectly. This program encourages the use of feedback and discussion to help students "think about their thinking."

After pupils begin to consider themselves "thinkers," they will be better able to learn and make use of content area material. Practicing skills such as identifying main ideas, classifying, identifying relationships, thinking about what will happen, and inferring will help students become better readers in the content areas.

Cognitive Skills

The first unit of study is **Knowledge**. This level is considered by many educators to be the first stage in cognitive development. This starting point includes both the acquisition of information and the ability to recall information when needed. The following skills are helpful in developing this stage:

1. Classifying
2. Discriminating Between Real and Make-Believe
3. Discriminating Between Fact and Opinion
4. Discriminating Between Definition and Example
5. Outlining and Summarizing

The second unit of study is **Comprehension**. Comprehension refers to the basic level of understanding and involves the ability to know what is being communicated in order to make use of the information. This includes translating or interpreting a communication or extrapolating information from a communication.

Critical Thinking 2, SV 6213-X

The following skills are helpful in developing this stage:

1. Comparing and Contrasting
2. Identifying Structure
3. Identifying Steps in a Process
4. Understanding Pictures
5. Identifying Main Ideas
6. Identifying Relationships

The third unit of study is **Application**. Application is the ability to use a learned skill in a new situation. The following skills are helpful in developing this stage:

1. Ordering Objects
2. Estimating
3. Thinking About What Will Happen
4. Inferring
5. Interpreting Changes in Word Meanings

The fourth unit of study is **Analysis**. Analysis is the ability to break down information into its integral parts and to identify the relationship of each part to the total organization. The following skills are helpful in developing this stage:

1. Judging Completeness
2. Thinking About Facts That Fit
3. Distinguishing Abstract from Concrete
4. Judging Logic of Actions
5. Identifying Parts of a Story
6. Examining Story Logic
7. Recognizing True and False

Features of the Program
Specific skills are listed in the Table of Contents and may be easily found if you need to access a certain skill or area. Each of the 24 skills has been correlated to the content areas of language arts, social studies, science, and math. This chart is on page 4. A letter to parents explaining the goals and benefits of the program is provided on page 5.

The Assessment Test on pages 6-7 may be used to gauge pupils' critical thinking abilities before and after completion of the program. Each unit is also followed by a two-page Assessment Test. The Student Mastery Checklist on page 8 will facilitate your record keeping.

* Bloom, Benjamin, *Taxonomy of Educational Objectives, Handbook 1: Cognitive Domain*, New York: David McKay Company, Inc., 1956.

CORRELATION TO CONTENT AREAS

Pages	Reading and Language Arts	Social Studies	Science	Math
9-13	✔	✔		
14-17	✔			
18-21	✔	✔		
22-25	✔		✔	
26-29	✔	✔	✔	
32-34		✔	✔	✔
35-36		✔	✔	
37-40	✔	✔		✔
41-42				✔
43-44	✔			
45-48	✔		✔	
49-52	✔	✔		
55-57				✔
58-61				✔
62-65	✔	✔		
66-69	✔	✔		
70-73	✔			
76-78	✔	✔		✔
79-80	✔	✔	✔	
81-83	✔			✔
84-86		✔		
87-88	✔	✔		
89-90	✔			
91-92	✔			

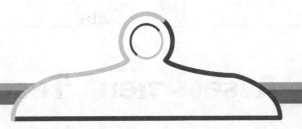

Dear Parent,

Being able to think clearly and process information in increasingly complex ways is a necessity in the modern world and one of the primary goals of education. This year your child will be using critical thinking exercises to extend his or her ability to read, think, and reason.

The skills we will be practicing are grouped in levels of thinking. These levels are knowledge, comprehension, application, and analysis. The levels are each important. The higher the level of thinking, the more complex the task is. The exercises move from the concrete to the more abstract levels of thinking. We will practice skills such as classifying, identifying main ideas, inferring, and judging completeness.

From time to time, your child may bring home some of these critical thinking practice sheets. To best help your child, please consider the following suggestions:

* Provide a quiet place to work.
* Go over the directions together.
* Show interest in the work.
* Encourage your child to do his or her best.
* Help your child if he or she gets frustrated.
* Check the lesson when it is complete.

Many of these exercises can be easily extended by thinking of similar examples. Your involvement will encourage your child, give you information about how he or she thinks, and provide an opportunity for you to work together. Positive family experiences such as these help promote life-long learning.

Thanks for your help!

Sincerely,

Assessment Test

A.   Thinking About What Will Happen

Read the first two parts of the poem. Then finish the poem using the lines in the **Rhyme Line Box**.

Count to **one**
The cake is **done**.

Count to **two**
Give it to **Sue**

Count to **three**
Serve it with tea.

Count to **four**
May we have more?

Rhyme Line Box

May we have more?
Serve it with tea.

B.   Definition and Example
Outlining and Summarizing

Finish the outline by writing the names of the animals that go with each definition. Use the **Word Box**.

I.   Wild animals used in circuses

   A. _____

   B. _____

II.   Tame animals used as pets

   A. _____

   B. _____

Word Box

giraffe
puppy
elephant
kitten

Assessment Test, p. 2

C. Identifying Relationships
Understanding Pictures

Draw a line from each sentence to the thing the animal needs.

The deer is thirsty.

The bird wants to build a nest.

The bee wants to fly home.

D. Steps in a Process
Identifying Main Ideas

The directions for building a doghouse are below, but they are all mixed up. Write **1** before the step that comes first, **2** before the second step, and so on.

_____ Build the roof.

_____ Get wood, hammers, and nails.

_____ Paint the doghouse.

_____ Build the sides of the house.

On the line below, write a title for your directions.

_____

Student Mastery Checklist

Name	Skill # 1	2	3	4	5	6	7	8	9	10	11	12	13	14	15	16	17	18	19	20	21	22	23	24	Comments

UNIT 1 Knowledge
Classifying

Find the pictures of two things that belong in each box. Write their letters on the lines in the box.

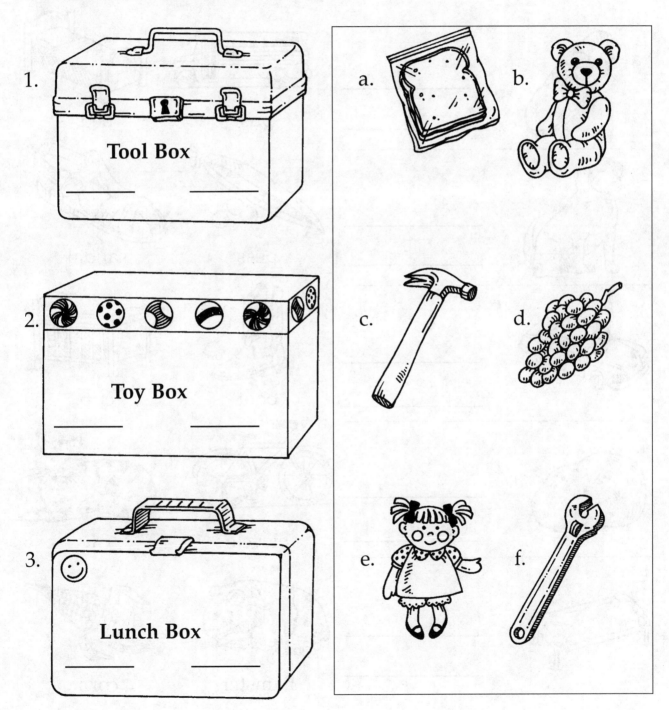

1. Tool Box
   _____ _____

2. Toy Box
   _____ _____

3. Lunch Box
   _____ _____

a.

b.

c.

d.

e.

f.

Classifying

Look at each numbered picture on the left. Find two pictures on the right that show something like it. Write their names on the lines.

1. _____

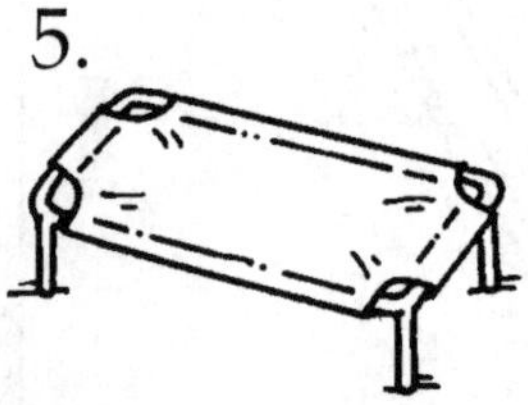

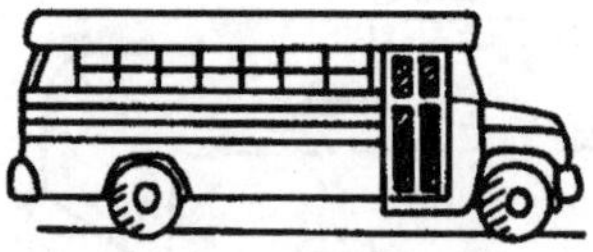

bus 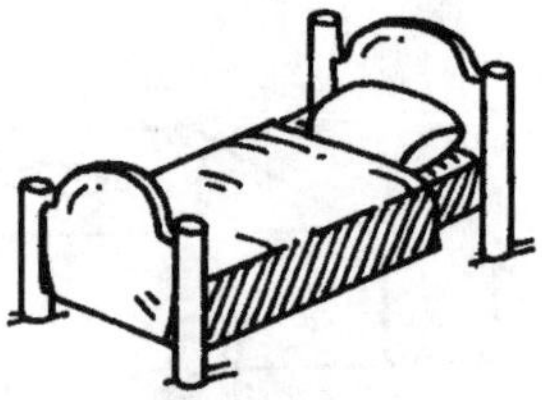   bed

2. _____

peas 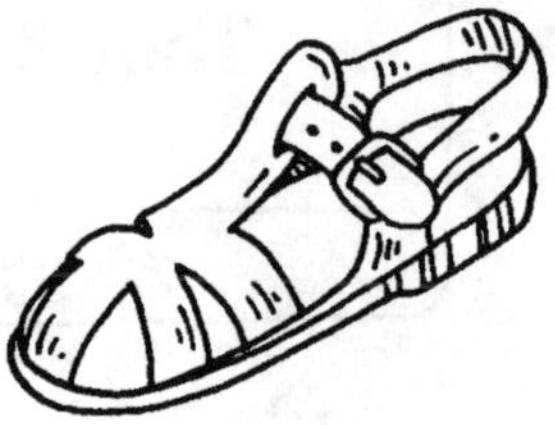   sandal

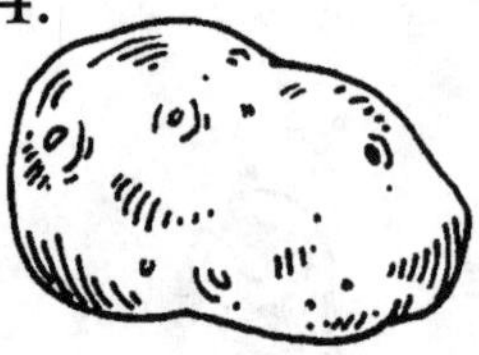

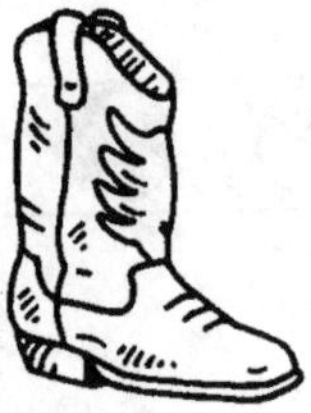

3. _____

boot    crib

4. _____

bicycle    cat

5. _____

hamster 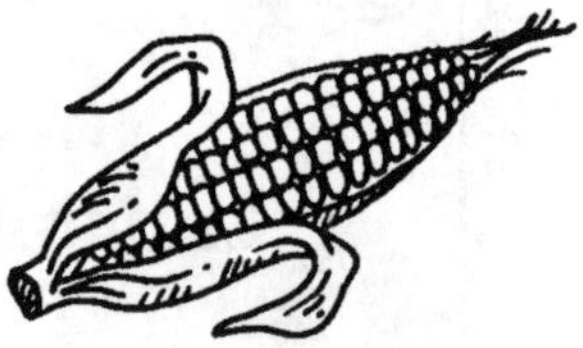   corn

Critical Thinking 2, SV 6213-X

Classifying

Where can you find the things written on the fish? Write each word under the hook that tells where each thing should go.

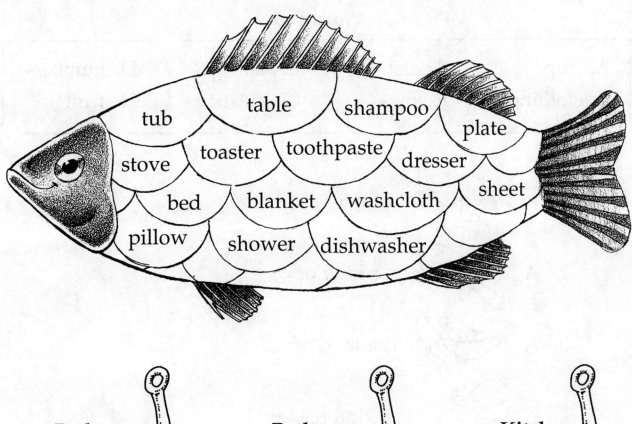

tub table shampoo plate
stove toaster toothpaste dresser
bed blanket washcloth sheet
pillow shower dishwasher

Bedroom   **Bathroom**   **Kitchen**

_____   _____   _____

_____   _____   _____

_____   _____   _____

_____   _____   _____

Classifying

Read each sentence. Find the word in the **Word Box** that fits in the blank. Write the letter of that word.

Word Box

A. bug	B. dish	C. car	D. numbers
E. clothing	F. toy	G. meat	H. fruit

1. A is one of a group of _____ .

2. A 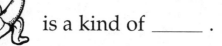 is a kind of _____ .

3. A 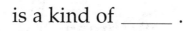 is a kind of _____ .

4. A is a kind of _____ .

5. A is a kind of _____ .

6. A is a kind of _____ .

7. A is a kind of _____ .

8. A is a kind of _____ .

                          Critical Thinking 2, SV 6213-X

Classifying

Find the two words that go with each picture. Write the letters of the two words on the lines.

1. A. bird
    B. chair
    C. top
    D. robin
    E. poodle
    F. furniture
    G. toy
    H. dog
    I. clothes
    J. jacket

2. A. tulip
    B. cat
    C. apple
    D. jewelry
    E. flower
    F. house
    G. fruit
    H. building
    I. animal
    J. ring

Critical Thinking 2, SV 6213-X

Real and Make-Believe

Circle the sentences that tell about something make-believe.
Put an **X** on the picture that shows something real.

1. Horses go to bed when they are sick.

2. Some trees grow upside down.

3. Some pigs have five legs and a cap.

4. A man and a boy can row a boat.

5. A squirrel can row a boat.

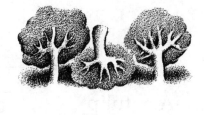

Critical Thinking 2, SV 6213-X

Real and Make-Believe

Put an **R** before the things that are real. Put an **M** before the things that are make-believe.

_____ 1. a blue elephant

_____ 2. a plant with thorns

_____ 3. a brown lizard

_____ 4. a purple leopard

_____ 5. a hen with legs four feet long

_____ 6. a pencil that writes with no help

_____ 7. a brown-and-white spotted cow

_____ 8. a dancing pig

_____ 9. a magic wand

_____ 10. a twenty-foot tall giant

_____ 11. orange raindrops

_____ 12. a cow that flies without a plane

_____ 13. a white rose

_____ 14. a three-foot-high apple

_____ 15. a chair that stays outside

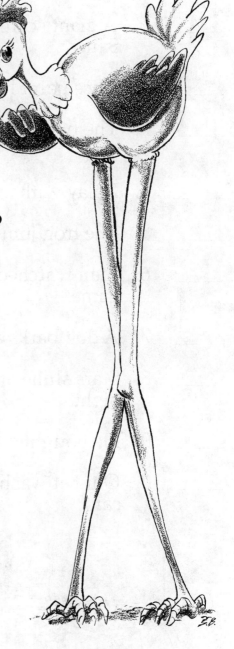

Real and Make-Believe

Write **M** if the sentence tells something make-believe. Write **R** if it tells something real. Then match each sentence to the left to one on the right that tells about the same thing.

__M__   1. A giant scared Sam.

_____   2. Mice paint houses.

_____   3. The pumpkin sang.

_____   4. I play with an elf.

_____   5. The frog jumped.

_____   6. Juan watched the game.

_____   7. A dog barks at me.

_____   8. Stars shine at night.

_____   9. He bought a pan.

_____   10. Our cat washes cars.

A. A frog became a prince.

B. We like pumpkin pie.

C. Stars fell on his head.

D. Giants are in the story.

E. The dog danced a polka.

F. Juan saw three goblins.

G. A cat washes its face.

H. Mice run in old houses.

I. The pan laughed loudly.

J. An elf was in my dream.

Critical Thinking 2, SV 6213-X

Real and Make-Believe

Ann

Mike

These children like to tell stories. Ann tells stories about things that really can happen. Mike likes to tell make-believe stories.

Copy each sentence below under the correct heading.

I saw a purple dog.
My sister tells funny stories.
My lizard has four legs.

My house is made of peanut butter.
I often drink milk while eating.
A sock gets hungry at lunchtime.

Real   **Make-believe**

_____   _____

_____   _____

_____   _____

_____   _____

_____   _____

Critical Thinking 2, SV 6213-X

Fact and Opinion

Write **F** before each sentence that tells a fact. Write **O** before each sentence that tells an opinion.

_____ 1. Rabbits run faster than turtles.

_____ 2. Pencils are used for writing.

_____ 3. This peach is the best peach in the world.

_____ 4. Climbing trees is not a good thing to do.

_____ 5. Dinosaurs lived long ago.

_____ 6. My kitten is prettier than your kitten.

_____ 7. Babies are smaller than mothers.

_____ 8. That juice is too sweet.

_____ 9. Hammers and saws are tools.

_____ 10. Some shoes are made of leather.

_____ 11. Bananas taste better than apples.

_____ 12. Cats are not as friendly as dogs.

_____ 13. There are many different kinds of cars.

_____ 14. That barn is too big and ugly.

_____ 15. Rob's picture is better than mine.

Fact and Opinion

A. Draw a line from each fact sentence to an opinion sentence on the same subject.

Facts

Opinions

1. Most people have hair.
2. Thanksgiving is a holiday.
3. Horses have four legs.
4. People need food.
5. Baseball is a game.
6. Bicycles have wheels.
7. A blue jay is a bird.
8. My mom drives to work.

A. Riding a horse is dangerous.
B. Lunch is the best meal of the day.
C. Blue jays are too noisy.
D. Red hair is the most beautiful.
E. Everyone should have a bicycle.
F. It's easy to drive a car.
G. Thanksgiving is the best day of all.
H. The rules of baseball are easy.

B. Look at the hat.
Then write two sentences of your own.

1. A **fact** about the hat:

_____

2. My **opinion** about the hat:

_____

Fact and Opinion

Read the story. Underline the three sentences that tell opinions.

Our class gave a Book Fair. We set up booths in the hallway. Each booth was for a different kind of book. I think the mystery story booth was the most interesting.

We made posters and signs for our Book Fair. I think my poster was the best one. Carol and Mike painted a sign that was bigger than any of the others.

Every class in the school visited the fair. It was the best Book Fair in the whole wide world!

Critical Thinking 2, SV 6213-X

Fact and Opinion

Finish the two sentences beside each picture. Make one sentence tell a fact. Make the other sentence tell your opinion.

Fact: The riders _____ .

Opinion: Biking is _____ .

Fact: The girls _____ .

Opinion: Jumping is _____ .

Fact: The boys _____ .

Opinion: I think _____ .

Fact: The children _____ .

Opinion: Camping is _____ .

Definition and Example

A. On each line, write the number of the correct word from the **Word Box**.

_____ grows on a tree

_____ lives but is not a plant

_____ holds many things inside

_____ holds water and other drinks

_____ something to play with

Word Box

1. animal
2. box
3. toy
4. leaf
5. cup

B. Which word in the **Word Box** goes with each picture? Write the number of the word on the line.

_____

_____

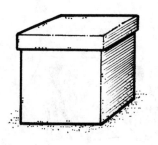

_____

_____

_____

Critical Thinking 2, SV 6213-X

· · · Definition and Example · · ·

A. On each line, write the number of the correct word from the **Word Box**.

Word Box

_____ These are growing things with leaves.

_____ These are part of the alphabet.

_____ You stay in them.

_____ It helps you to grow.

1. food
2. letters
3. plants
4. buildings

B. On each line, write the number of a word from the **Word Box**. You will use each number more than once.

   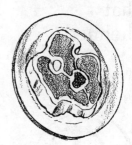

_____ _____ _____

_____ _____ _____

Definition and Example

Read each definition and the examples. Circle the word that names the example shown in the picture.

1. a covering for the head

   scarf
   hat
   helmet

2. an animal with wings

   butterfly
   bird
   bat

3. a tool for writing

   crayon
   pencil
   pen

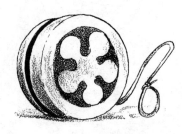

4. a round toy

   yoyo
   marble
   ball

5. a yellow fruit

   banana
   lemon
   pear

6. a sea animal

   seal
   fish
   dolphin

Critical Thinking 2, SV 6213-X

Definition and Example

Read the word under each picture. Write the word under the correct definition.

1. a tool for writing

   _____

   _____

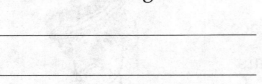  

swan   hammer

2. a tool used by builders

   _____

   _____

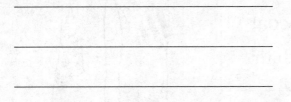  

pencil   duck

nail   saw

3. a bird that can swim

   _____

   _____

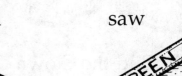 

pen   crayon

pelican

Critical Thinking 2, SV 6213-X

Outlining and Summarizing

Look at the two clowns. Write words from the box to tell about each clown.

big hat
happy face
big pants
short
tall
no hair
sad face
tiny hat
small coat
curly hair

Bud the Clown

Babs the Clown

1. _____

2. _____

3. _____

4. _____

5. _____

1. _____

2. _____

3. _____

4. _____

5. _____

Critical Thinking 2, SV 6213-X

Outlining and Summarizing

Read each story. Then write the most important words from the story on the lines below.

1. Shep is a big dog. He stays outside. He chases cars. He barks at the squirrels. Ted plays with Shep.

2. Mitten is a black kitten. She has white feet. She stays in the house. She sleeps in a chair. She drinks milk. She purrs.

1. Shep

    is a big dog

    _____

    chases cars

    _____

    _____

2. Mitten

    _____

    has white feet

    _____

    _____

    drinks milk

    _____

Outlining and Summarizing

Read each part of the story. Write the answer to each question on the line that comes after it.

The Children's Pets

Tom has a baby duck. It is little and fluffy. It is yellow. The duck says quack.

What is Tom's pet?   I. _____

What size is it?   A. _____

What does it feel like?   B. _____

What color is it?   C. _____

What does it say?   D. _____

Pam has a tiny turtle. Its shell is hard. Its body is soft. It hides its head inside the shell.

What is Pam's pet?   II. _____

What size is it?   A. _____

What covers it?   B. _____

What is soft?   C. _____

Where does it hide its head?   D. _____

Outlining and Summarizing

Read the story. Then fill in the lines on the outline. On each line, tell something about that kind of home.

Native American Homes

The Pueblo people lived in homes called **pueblos**. These homes were made of sun-dried earth called **adobe**. The roof of one was the floor of another.

Navajo people lived in homes called **hogans**. Hogans were made of logs covered with earth. They had dome-shaped roofs.

Native American Homes

I. Pueblo homes

   A. _____

   B. _____

II. Navajo homes

   A. _____

   B. _____

pueblo

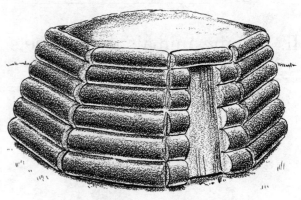

hogan

Critical Thinking 2, SV 6213-X

Name _____   Date _____

Unit 1 Assessment Test

A. Classifying

Help! The circus wagon broke down! All the animals ran into the pet shop. Circle the animals that belong to the circus. Draw an **X** on the pet shop animals.

B. Definition and Example
Outlining and Summarizing

Finish the outline by writing the names of the animals that go with each definition. Use the **Word Box**.

I. Wild animals used in circuses

    A. _____

    B. _____

II. Tame animals used as pets

    A. _____

    B. _____

Word Box

giraffe

puppy

elephant

kitten

Critical Thinking 2, SV 6213-X

Unit 1 Assessment Test, p. 2

C. **Fact and Opinion**
    Real and Make-Believe

Read the poems. Write **fact, opinion,** or **make-believe**.

A little egg
in a nest of hay.
Cheep-cheep.
Crack-crack.
A little chick
pecked his shell away.
Cheep-cheep.
Crack-crack.

_____

A little white mouse
Playing on a sunbeam,
Then sliding back down.

_____

I am a nice boy.
More than just nice,
Two million times more,
The word is ADORABLE.

_____

Look at the picture.
What do you see?
What can you
imagine? Put your
ideas into a poem.
Write it on a sheet
of paper.

Unit 2 Comprehension
Comparing and Contrasting

For each row, write the letter of the one that is different.

1.   A   B   C   D   ____

2.   A   B   C   D   ____

3.   A   B   C   D   ____

4.   A   B   C   D   ____

5.   A   B   C   D   ____

6.   A   B   C   D   ____

Critical Thinking 2, SV 6213-X

Comparing and Contrasting

Read each question. Put a line under the best answer.

1. How are teachers, farmers, and doctors alike?
   They all work outdoors.   They are all people.
   They all go to school.

2. How are cabins, houses, and tents alike?
   They can be moved.   They all have fireplaces.
   You can live in them.

3. How are palm trees, apple trees, and grass alike?
   They are very tall.   They stay green all winter.
   They are plants.

4. How are kittens, calves, and puppies alike?
   They are young animals.   They are house pets.
   They are the same size.

5. How are trucks, tractors, and cars alike?
   They all stay outdoors.   They all have wheels.
   They are used only on farms.

6. How are chalk, pencils, and pens alike?
   They are used for writing.   They are all sharp.
   They all have erasers on them.

7. How are scissors, needles, and thread alike?
   They all cut.   They are used for sewing.
   They are all used for cooking.

Comparing and Contrasting

On each blank like, write a word from the **Word Box**.

Word Box

birds	beak	little	two	short

Both of these animals are _____ . One bird is big. The

other bird is _____ . One bird has long feathers. The other

bird has _____ feathers.

Each bird has _____ feet and a _____ .

Identifying Structure

A. Houses have special parts outside. Look at the parts listed below. Write the number of each part to show where it belongs on the house.

1. door   4. window
2. roof   5. steps
3. brick   6. chimney

B. Houses also have special parts inside. Here is the inside of a house. Write the number of each part on the picture to show where it belongs.

1. ceiling   4. curtains
2. floor   5. fireplace
3. wall   6. bookcase

C. Write a word from the **Word Box** in each blank.

Word Box

carpet	paint	tile	wallpaper

Cover the inside walls of a house with _____ or

_____ . Cover the floors with _____ or

_____ .

Critical Thinking 2, SV 6213-X   **35**

Identifying Structure

A. Different words may use the same letters. The order of the letters is different in these words: **tea, ate**. For each Pet Shop Word below, make another word. Use all the letters. The first one is done for you.

Pet Show Word	Another Word
1. shop	1. hops
2. owl	2. _____
3. yap	3. _____
4. nip	4. _____

B. With some words, you can change one letter to make a new word. Change just one letter in each word on the Dog Word list to make another word that goes with the definition. The first one is done for you.

Dog Word	Definition	New Word
1. puppy	a kind of flower	1. poppy
2. fur	belonging to us	2. _____
3. bark	a farm building	3. _____
4. ball	something to ring	4. _____

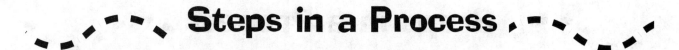

Steps in a Process

Read the story. Number the pictures in order.

On Saturday morning, Jimmy got up, brushed his teeth, and got dressed. Mother said that breakfast was ready. Jimmy ate breakfast. Then he played outdoors with his sister Alice. When Leon came along, all three children played together.

_____   _____

_____   _____

Steps in a Process

Read the story. Then number the pictures in order. Use the numbers
1, 2, 3, 4, and **5**.

Inez decided to make a sock puppet. She used an old sock
that she found in her drawer. She cut dog ears out of a piece
of brown felt. She glued one ear on each side of the sock. With
red and brown markers, she drew a dog mouth and nose on
the sock. Then she glued on two blue buttons for eyes. When
the glue was dry, Inez put her hand in the sock and used her
puppet to tell a story.

_____   _____   _____

_____   _____

Critical Thinking 2, SV 6213-X

Steps in a Process

Write **1**, **2**, and **3** to tell each story in order.

A. ____ Liz wanted to ride her new bike.

____ She rode over to see her friend.

____ The two friends rode bikes.

B. ____ Tom and Jay picked some fruit.

____ That night the family ate fruit salad.

____ Mother cut up the fruit and made a fruit salad.

C. ____ Carla began to dance.

____ Carla put on her leotards.

____ She found her favorite music record.

D. ____ They bought a western shirt.

____ They looked for a shirt for Bob.

____ Bob and his father went to the store.

E. ____ Ann hung the picture in her room.

____ She drew a picture of a horse.

____ Ann took out her crayons and paper.

Steps in a Process

Look at the story pictures and read the sentences in a box. Then write the sentences to show what happened first, second, and third.

A. | Tina made a sign and put it up.   Tina built the fort.
Tina got the things to build a fort.

1. _____

2. _____

3. _____

B. | The kitten got stuck in a tree.   He rescued the kitten.
Uncle Carlos brought a ladder.

1. _____

2. _____

3. _____

Critical Thinking 2, SV 6213-X

Name _____ Date _____

Understanding Pictures

Color this shape ▢ green.   Color this shape ◯ orange.

Color this shape △ brown.   Color this ▢ and this ▢ yellow.

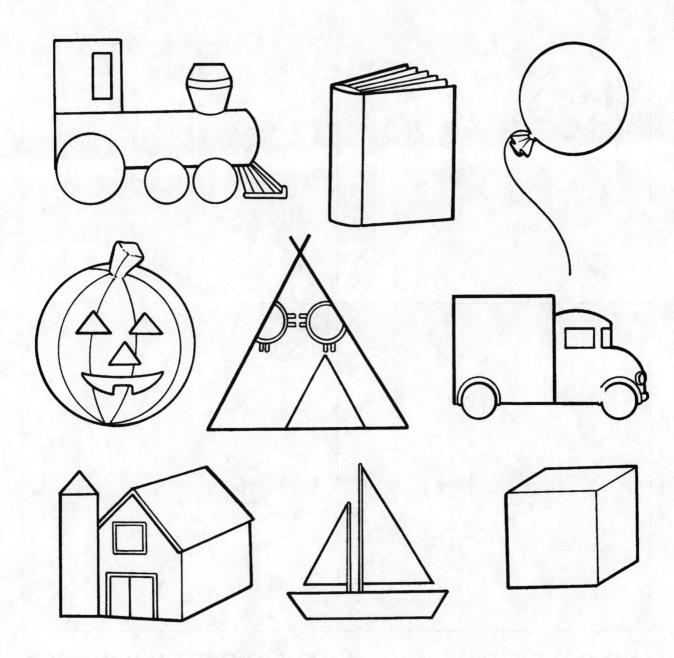

Understanding Pictures

Fourteen letters of the alphabet with straight lines are hiding here! Find the E and trace it with your finger. Circle it in the alphabet below. Then find the other letters.

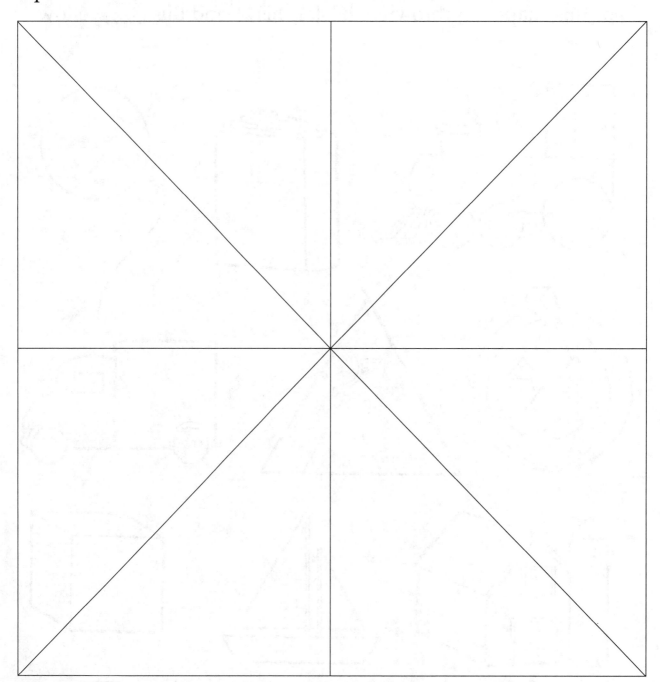

A B C D E F G H I J K L M N O P Q R S T U V W X Y Z

Comparing Word Meanings

Write the word that means the same. Then write the word that means the opposite.

		Same	**Opposite**

A. | bad | same | bold | nice | afraid | different |

1. brave _____   _____

2. alike _____   _____

3. good _____   _____

B. | dull | mend | big | shining | small | smash |

1. little _____   _____

2. bright _____   _____

3. break _____   _____

C. | well | fast | tall | slow | short | ill |

1. high _____   _____

2. quick _____   _____

3. sick _____   _____

Critical Thinking 2, SV 6213-X   **43**

Comparing Word Meanings

In each blank, write the correct word from the **Word Box**.

Word Box

be	rode	flour	would	two	wood
to	road	bee	sun	flower	son

Examples: He is the youngest __son__ of the family.

The ___sun___ is bright today.

1. May we go _____ the store?

2. Twins are _____ children who often look alike.

3. Jane _____ the horse for a long time.

4. The car was on the _____ .

5. A tulip is a kind of _____ .

6. I use _____ when I bake.

7. Lee wants to _____ a teacher.

8. The _____ stung me on the arm.

9. We _____ like to go with you.

10. The chair is made of _____ .

Critical Thinking 2, SV 6213-X

Identifying Main Ideas

Circle the best title for each story.

A.   Spot is a little gray pony. He lives on a farm. One day, Mei was riding Spot. Spot stepped into a hole. He hurt his leg. The doctor had to fix it.

1. Spot's Hurt Leg
2. Mei Loves Spot
3. A Little Gray Pony

B.   The turtle and the hippo had a race. The hippo went faster than the turtle. It finished the race before the turtle did. The turtle said, "I enjoyed our race."

1. Angry Turtle
2. The Speedy Hippo
3. The Elephant's Friend

C.   People keep many kinds of pets in their homes. Some have dogs or cats. Others have birds or fish. Some people even have tame monkeys!

1. Sally's Pets
2. People Need Pets
3. Kinds of House Pets

Critical Thinking 2, SV 6213-X

·- · · Identifying Main Ideas · - · ·

Read each story. Then underline the sentence in the box that tells the main idea.

1.   A cactus is a spiny plant. It grows in the desert. It needs very little water.

| It is hot in the desert. |
| Cactus is a desert plant. |

2.   Oranges grow on trees. First they are green. Then they turn yellow. At last they turn orange.

| Oranges change color. |
| Oranges are juicy. |

3.   The part of a carrot that you eat is the root. It grows under the ground. It has lacy green leaves on top.

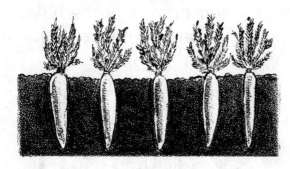

| Carrots taste good. |
| Carrots are root vegetables. |

4.   Cotton grows in places where it is hot. It needs lots of sunshine and water. When the cotton pods get very big, they burst open.

| Some clothes are made of cotton. |
| Cotton needs warm weather. |

                    Critical Thinking 2, SV 6213-X

Identifying Main Ideas

Read each story. Circle the sentence that tells the main idea.

1. Jackie tied on her bonnet. Then she laced up her high-top shoes. Jackie was getting ready for a costume party.

2. The parade was so much fun! We saw floats and banners. There were clowns and bands. There were even dancing dogs.

3. First you see streaks of light. Then the sky gets lighter and lighter. A sunrise is very beautiful.

4. Mark wanted to paint a picture. He set up his easel and paints. He found paper and brushes. Then he spread paper on the floor.

⸚⸚⸚ ⸗ ⸗ ⸗ Identifying Main Ideas ⸗ ⸗ ⸗ ⸚⸚⸚

Circle the word that tells what the story is about. Then draw a line under the main idea sentence.

Examples: (Kites) are lots of fun. You have to run fast to get them flying. Then the kites dance in the air.

1.   Here is how to make a mask. Get a big paper bag. Then use scissors to cut eyeholes. Use paint and yarn to finish the funny face.

2.   Skyrockets are beautiful. Their colors flash in the night sky. People enjoy watching the colors pop and drop through the dark.

3.   Tadpoles are young frogs. At first they look more like fish than frogs. They wiggle through the water. Soon they grow legs and can hop on the ground.

4.   Ben got a surprise for his birthday. The surprise was gray and white. The surprise said, "Meow." Ben gave the surprise a bowl of milk.

5.   Nancy filled the washtub with water. Next she found Bowser's soap and tub toy. Nancy was going to give her dog a bath.

6.   The sun gives us light. It makes the air warm. It helps things grow. The sun is important to everything on Earth.

Identifying Relationships

Write a number to show where each person is going.

_____   _____

_____   _____

_____   _____

Identifying Relationships

Read each job name in the middle. Draw lines to show two things used by a person who does that job.

   • **police officer** •

   • **firefighter** •

   • **chef** •

   • **carpenter** •

   • **astronaut** •

   • **nurse** •

Critical Thinking 2, SV 6213-X

Identifying Relationships

Write the letter of the picture that will fill each blank correctly.

A   B   C   D

E   F   G   H

1. It is raining, so you will need an ____ if you go out.

2. If you want to color, you will need ____ .

3. If you drop the ____ , it will break.

4. Some people like to read, so they need ____ .

5. If the ____ shines, the ____ will melt.

6. To catch a ____ , you need a ____ .

Critical Thinking 2, SV 6213-X   **51**

Identifying Relationships

Read each sentence. Fill in each blank with the correct word from the **Word Box**.

Word Box

Tuesday	bat	pencil	nail	hungry	water
baseball	won	apple	out	party	red

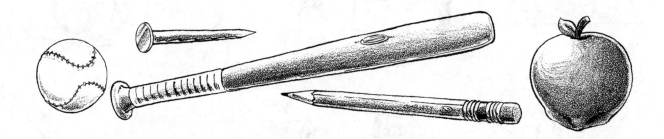

1. Eva ran faster than Sam, so Eva _____ the race.

2. Ben stepped on a rusty _____ , so he went to the doctor.

3. Since the sun is _____ , we can go on a picnic.

4. Tina wanted to write, so she got a _____ .

5. It was John's birthday, so we gave him a _____ .

6. Yesterday was Monday, so today must be _____ .

7. Lucy lost her green socks, so she wore her _____ ones.

8 If you are thirsty, drink some _____ .

9. To play _____ , you need a _____ .

10. Paul was _____ , so he ate an _____ .

  Critical Thinking 2, SV 6213-X

Name _____ Date _____

Unit 2 Assessment Test

A. **Identifying Relationships**
   Understanding Pictures

Draw a line from each sentence to the thing the animal needs.

The deer is thirsty.

The bird wants to build a nest.

The bee wants to fly home.

B. **Steps in a Process**
   Identifying Main Ideas

   The directions for building a doghouse are below, but they are all mixed up. Write **1** before the step that comes first, **2** before the second step, and so on.

____ Build the roof.

____ Get wood, hammers, and nails.

____ Paint the doghouse.

____ Build the sides of the house.

On the line below, write a title for your directions.

_____

Unit 2 Assessment Test, p. 2

C. **Identifying Structure**

An animal name is hiding in each of the words below. Circle the letters that name the animal. The first one is done for you.

1. b(o x)

2. c r a t e

3. c a p e

4. h e e l

5. s p i g o t

6. l a n t e r n

D. **Comparing and Contrasting**
    Comparing Word Meanings

You can write some words so that they **look** like what they mean.

In the space below, write the following word pairs so they look like what they mean.

beautiful ugly   happy sad   straight bent

Unit 3 Application
Ordering Objects

Put the pictures in each row in order. The first picture has **1** under it. Write **2**, **3**, and **4** on the correct lines.

A.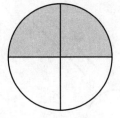

_____   _____   _____   __1__

B.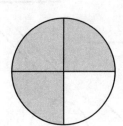

_____   _____   __1__   _____

C.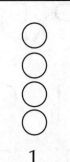

_____   __1__   _____   _____

D.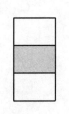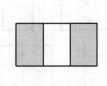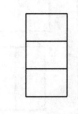

_____   _____   __1__   _____

Ordering Objects

For each row decide what comes next. Draw it.

1. 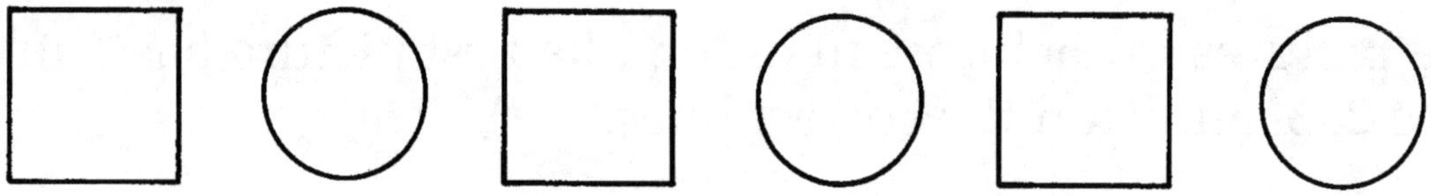 □ ○ □ ○ □ ○

2. 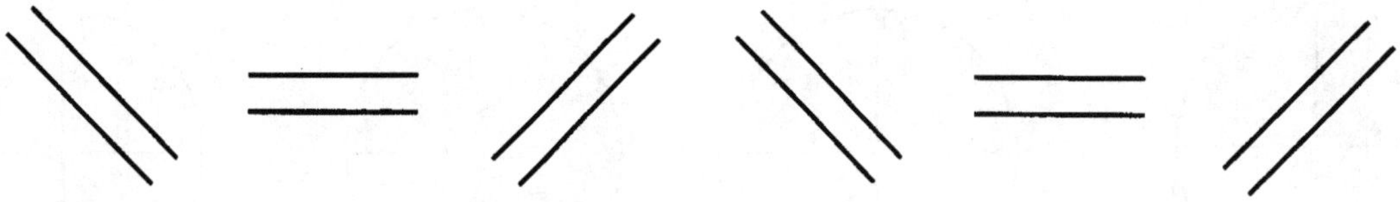 ∥ = ∥ ∖ = ∥

3. 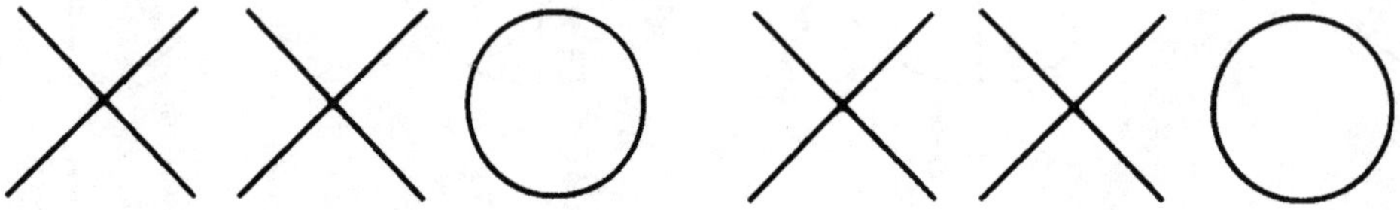 ✗ ✗ ○ ✗ ✗ ○

4. L M N O P Q R

5.

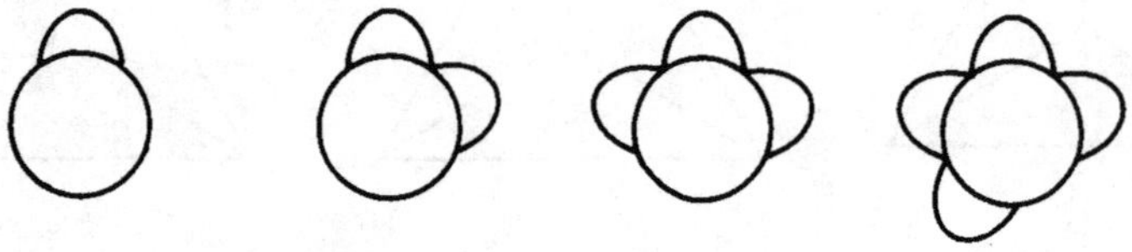

6. PxA PxB PxC PxD

7. 19 17 15 13 11 9

8.

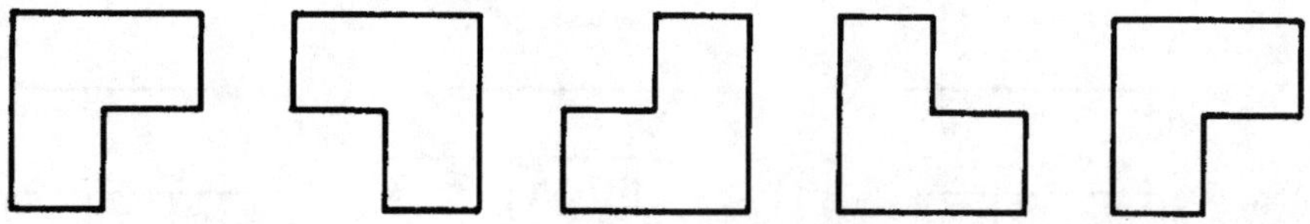

9.

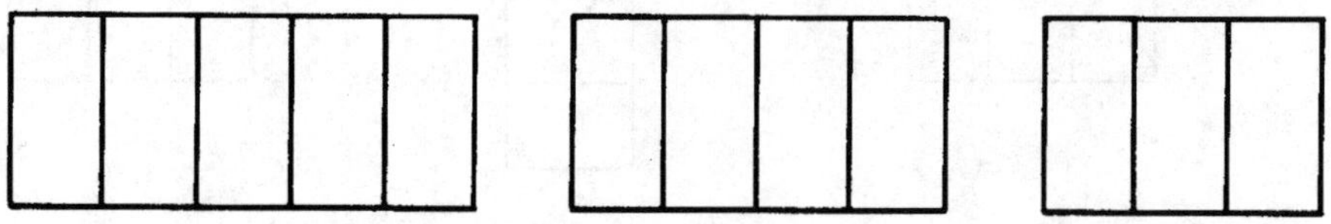

Critical Thinking 2, SV 6213-X

Ordering Objects

For each row, draw step 3.

A.

  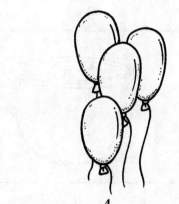

1.　　　　　　2.　　　　　　3.　　　　　　4.

B.

1.　　　　　　2.　　　　　　3.　　　　　　4.

C.

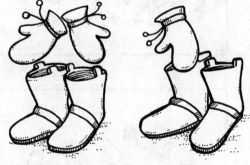 

1.　　　　　　2.　　　　　　3.　　　　　　4.

Estimating

Will the things pictured on the right fit into the container? If so, mark **X** on the line.

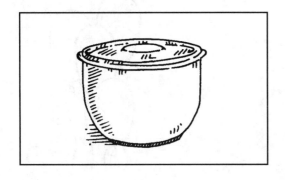 _____

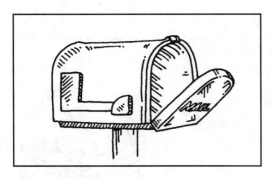 _____

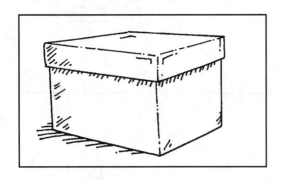 _____

 _____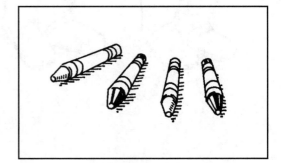

 Critical Thinking 2, SV 6213-X

Estimating

Circle the picture that answers each question.

1. Which ball will fit in the box?

2. What mitten will fit best?

3. Which drapes will fit best on the window?

4. Which tie will fit best on the shirt?

5. Which saucer will fit best with the cup?

6. Which collar will fit best on the dog?

7. Which box will fit on the shelf?

Estimating

Study the map. Then answer the questions.

1. Whose house is closest to the store?

   _____

2. Whose house is farthest from the school?

   _____

3. Which is closer to the school—the pond or the park?

   _____

4. Whose house is farthest from the restaurant?

   _____

5. Who lives across the street from the post office and the library?

   _____

Estimating

Circle the answer in each box that tells how long it would probably take to do each thing.

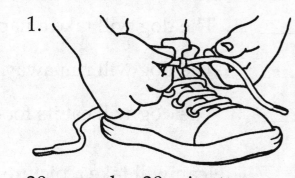

1. 30 seconds   30 minutes

2. 30 minutes   8 hours

3. 2 years   7 days

4. 3 seconds   2 minutes

5. 15 minutes   6 hours

6. 10 seconds   4 minutes

Thinking About What Will Happen

Look at each set of pictures. Then read the three sentences.
Put an **X** before the sentence that tells what will happen next.

A.

_____ 1. The dog will take a nap.

_____ 2. The dog will run away.

_____ 3. The dog will eat its food.

B.

_____ 1. Jean will take a picture.

_____ 2. Jean will ask someone to take a picture.

_____ 3. Jean has a camera that does not work.

C.

_____ 1. Hugo will play a game.

_____ 2. Hugo will color a picture.

_____ 3. Hugo will write a story.

D.

_____ 1. Her family will eat the plant.

_____ 2. Her family will enjoy the flowers.

_____ 3. Sue will throw the flowers away.

Critical Thinking 2, SV 6213-X

Thinking About What Will Happen

Read the beginning of each sentence. Circle the correct sentence ending.

1. If you plant a seed, it should

   die.   get smaller.   grow.   blow away.

2. When you write a word, you want others to

   read it.   cross it out.   erase it.   lose it.

3. When you go to a party, you want to

   be sad.   get sick.   go home.   have fun.

4. If you pack a suitcase, you are ready to

   go on a trip.   go to school.   eat.   get lost.

5. Pretend the temperature is zero. You will be

   hot.   warm.   cold.   cool.

6. If you lose some money, you will be

   sad.   glad.   happy.   tired.

7 When your team wins, you feel

   good.   bad.   silly.   sorry.

8. If you get a letter from a friend, you will

   lose it.   drop it.   find it.   read it.

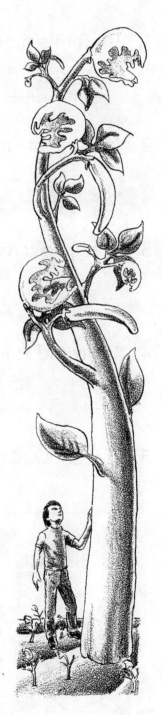

Thinking About What Will Happen

Read each sentence beginning. Finish the sentence in your own way.

1. If rabbits moved into my house, I would _____

_____.

2. If a dog ate my boots, I would _____

_____.

3. If a space creature came to my house, I would _____

_____.

4. If I could ride in the space shuttle, I would _____

_____.

5. If it snowed on the Fourth of July, I would _____

_____.

Critical Thinking 2, SV 6213-X

Thinking About What Will Happen

Put on your thinking cap! Ready? OK. Write sentences to answer these questions.

1. Do you think life on the earth would change if it stayed light 24 hours a day? How?

   _____

   _____

   _____

2. If it never rained again, would it change the way we live? How?

   _____

   _____

   _____

3. How would our lives change if we no longer had cars or buses or trains or planes?

   _____

   _____

   _____

Inferring

Write **yes** if you are sure that the sentence is true. Write **no** if you cannot be sure that the sentence is true.

1.

This ring could belong only to Jane. _____

2.

Mary lives in this apartment house. _____

3.

It is winter. _____

4.

The black horse will win. _____

5.

Meili caught this fish. _____

6.

The boy is riding the bicycle. _____

Inferring

Read each story. Circle the picture that answers the question at the end of the story. Then put an **X** before the sentence that tells why you chose that picture.

A.   John was watching a TV show. A man was crossing the desert. John could almost feel the hot sun. Soon, John ran to get something he wanted very much. What do you think it was?

What makes you think so?

1. ____   When you cross a desert, you need something to ride on.

2. ____   John was thirsty. He felt as if he were trying to cross the desert, too.

3. ____   John was tired of watching TV and wanted to play.

B.   Mother needed to go shopping. She had a list and her purse. Mother got into the car. She could not start it. She asked Lupe to get something for her. What did Mother want Lupe to get?

What makes you think so?

1. ____   Mother wanted to buy toys.

2. ____   The box can carry the groceries.

3. ____   You need a key to start a car.

Inferring

Read each story. Then follow the directions.

A.   A woman left some letters at Dot's house. One was from Dot's uncle. Circle the name of the person who left the letters.

Put an **X** in front of the reason for your choice.

| Dot's uncle |
| the mail carrier |
| Dot |

1. _____   Dot lives there.

2. _____   Dot's uncle wrote the letter.

3. _____   The mail carrier delivers mail to houses.

B.   Jack said, "What am I thinking of? The animal has little front legs, long back legs, and a pocket. It hops around on its back legs." Circle the name of the animal Jack is thinking of.

Put an **X** in front of the reason for your choice.

| a rabbit |
| a monkey |
| a kangaroo |

1. _____   Monkeys have four long legs for swinging.

2. _____   Rabbits have strong back legs and long ears.

3. _____   Kangaroos have strong back legs and a pocket.

Inferring

Read each story. In the blank, write the correct word from the story.

1. Carlos was walking down the street. He saw something fall from a girl's purse. He found a dime on the sidewalk.

   A _____ fell from the purse.

2. Father told Sue to finish her work after dinner. Sue finished dinner. Now she has to finish her _____.

3. Tomatoes must be picked as soon as they ripen. The tomatoes are ripe now. They must be _____.

4. On Wednesday the school lunchroom serves pizza. Today is Wednesday. The children will have _____ for lunch.

5. Frank must shovel snow before he plays. He has shoveled the snow. Now Frank can _____.

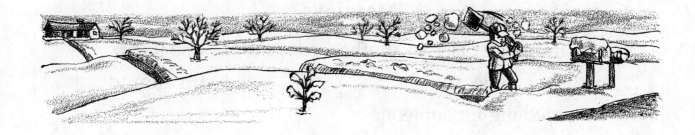

Changes in Word Meanings

Read each sentence. Think about how the word **run** is used. Find that meaning in the box. Write its number on the line after the sentence.

A.

The stream runs under the bridge. _____

B.

Our house is on her run. _____

C.

Windmills can run. _____

D.

They can run an errand. _____

E.
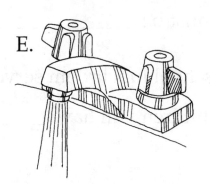
The faucet runs. _____

F.

The boy runs. _____

Meanings

1. goes from one place to another
2. the water comes out
3. do something for someone
4. usual trip
5. go around
6. goes fast

Critical Thinking 2, SV 6213-X

Changes in Word Meanings

Read the words and their meanings. Then read each sentence. Put the letter of the correct meaning for each underlined word in front of each sentence.

Word Meanings

<u>fly</u>	A.	insect with wings
	B.	move through the air with wings
<u>roll</u>	A.	kind of bread
	B.	turn over and over
<u>ring</u>	A.	give out a sound
	B.	thin circle of metal

_____ The <u>fly</u> landed on the flower.

_____ Birds <u>fly</u> south in the winter.

_____ Dad gave me a <u>ring</u> for my birthday.

_____ Did the phone <u>ring</u>?

_____ Maria wants a <u>roll</u> with her dinner.

_____ Let's <u>roll</u> down the hill.

Changes in Word Meanings

Read each sentence. Find a word in the **Word Box** that has the same meaning as the underlined words. Write the word on the line.

Word Box

| left | give | finished | help | come | watch | borrowed |

1. Mike <u>took out</u> a book. _____

2. Tina will <u>lend a hand</u>. _____

3. <u>Hand over</u> the jump rope to Jan. _____

4. Please <u>keep an eye on</u> the baby. _____

5. The airplane <u>took off</u>. _____

6. The game is <u>all over</u>. _____

7. Night has <u>fallen</u>. _____

Critical Thinking 2, SV 6213-X

Changes in Word Meanings

Write a word from the box to finish each sentence. When you finish the story, go back and circle the correct meaning of each word.

bill	A. bird's beak	B. list of what is owed
pet	A. stroke or pat	B. animal kept by a person
left	A. opposite of right	B. went away from
pen	A. something for writing	B. fenced place for animals
line	A. long, thin mark	B. straight row

Miss Cody's class was excited. They were going to visit the children's zoo. They stood in a long _____ with other people at the gate. Once inside, they saw all kinds of animals. They went into a wooden _____ where there were friendly sheep. They admired the big bright _____ of a toucan in a huge bird cage. They even got to gently _____ a baby rabbit. They were very tired when they finally _____ the zoo at the day's end.

Name _____ **Date** _____

Unit 3 Assessment Test

A. **Ordering Objects**
    Estimating
    Inferring

1. The boat race is about to start! First, the boats must line up according to size. Write **1** on the smallest boat, **2** on the next smallest, and so on up to **6**.

2. Look at **Zip** and **Princess**. Which one uses more gas?

    _____

    Tell why you think so. _____

3. Look at **Flipper** and **Plug**. Which one can go faster if just one

    person is in it? _____

    Tell why you think so. _____

Unit 3 Assessment Test, p. 2

B. Thinking About What Will Happen

Read the first two parts of the poem. Then finish the poem using the lines in the **Rhyme Line Box**.

Count to **one**
The cake is **done**.

Count to **two**
Give it to **Sue**

Count to **three**

_____

Count to **four**

_____

Rhyme Line Box

May we have more?
Serve it with tea.

C. Changes in Word Meanings

It's fun to make up new words. Look at the new word one writer made up. Then make up your own new words to go in the sentences.

A **neckle** is a freckle on your neck.

1. The place where lost socks go is a _____.

2. The button on top of a baseball cap is a _____.

Unit 4 Analysis

· · · Judging Completeness · · ·

Finish drawing each picture.

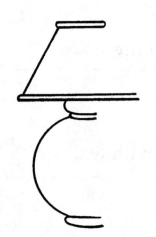

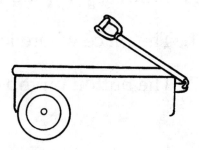

 Critical Thinking 2, SV 6213-X

Judging Completeness

Read each sentence. Study the picture. Complete the sentence with a word from the **Word Box**.

Word Box

hands	wheel	door	picture	handle	short

1. The frame has no

   _____ .

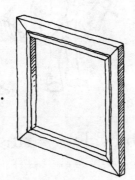

2. The wagon needs a

   _____ .

3. One leg is too

   _____ .

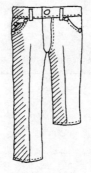

4. The pitcher needs a

   _____ .

5. The house has no

   _____ .

6. The clock has no

   _____ .

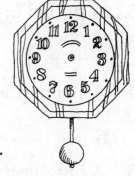

Critical Thinking 2, SV 6213-X

Judging Completeness

A word is missing from each sentence below. Add a word from the box to complete each sentence and to tell about the picture. Write the new sentence.

magician	acrobats	bicycle	rings	wire

1. A little clown rode a huge.

   _____

2. Three strong made a pyramid.

   _____

3. A pulled an umbrella from a top hat.

   _____

4. A woman walked on a up in the air.

   _____

5. A juggler threw high into the air.

   _____

Thinking About Facts That Fit

For each part, put an **X** before the two things you feel are most important.

1. You are going to a friend's birthday party. You need to know

   _____ where the party will be.

   _____ what time the party will be.

   _____ how many people will be there.

2. You are going to the circus. You need to know

   _____ how to get there.

   _____ why a circus has animals.

   _____ how much it will cost.

3. You want to make a garden. You should know

   _____ how many of your friends eat vegetables.

   _____ how to plant a seed.

   _____ how often to water the garden.

4. Your friend will make a valentine. He will need

   _____ paste and scissors.

   _____ some kind of paper.

   _____ a book telling about holidays.

Thinking About Facts That Fit

A. Read the story.

Carol was going on a trip with her family. Who would take care of her little brown hamster while she was gone?

"I'll be glad to do that for you," said Carol's friend Lee.

Carol took her hamster to Lee's house. "This hamster's name is Wheelo," said Carol. "That's because his favorite toy is this wheel he runs around on. The main thing is to keep Wheelo healthy. He needs food three times a day. He needs water all the time. He has to be in a warm place."

"What's this little cage for?" asked Lee.

"You have to clean Wheelo's cage twice a week," said Carol. "Put him in the little cage while you clean his big one."

B.   Put an **X** before the four most important rules.

Taking Care of a Hamster

1. ____ Feed it on time.

2. ____ Know the hamster's name.

3. ____ Keep the hamster warm.

4. ____ Give the hamster a wheel.

5. ____ Know the color of the hamster.

6. ____ Make sure the hamster has water.

7. ____ Play with the hamster.

8. ____ Clean the cage.

Name _____ Date _____

- - - - Abstract or Concrete - - - -

Study the **Word Box**. On the lines in part 1, write words that name things you can only **think** about. In part 2, write words that name things you can **touch**.

Word Box

scarf	flower
pretty	button
silly	happy
mean	fish
idea	funny
angry	crayon
ball	busy
egg	bicycle
pen	kitten
lazy	pencil

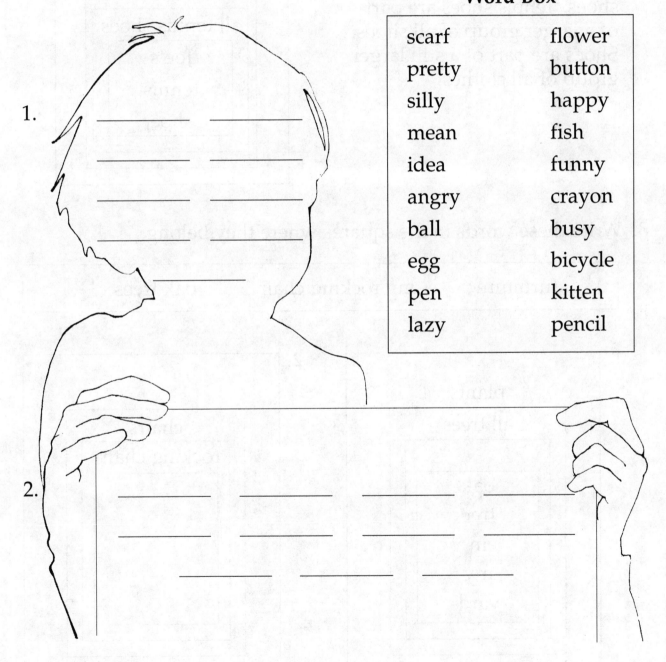

1.

2.

Critical Thinking 2, SV 6213-X

Abstract or Concrete

A. Look at the square at the right. Read about what it shows.

Joe's tennis shoe is part of a larger group of all tennis shoes. Tennis shoes are part of a larger group of all shoes. Shoes are part of a still larger group of all clothes.

B. Write these words in the squares where they belong.

| furniture | my rocking chair | oak trees |

1.

plants

all trees

oak

tree

in

my

yard

2.

chairs

rocking chairs

Critical Thinking 2, SV 6213-X

Abstract or Concrete

Read the words in the squares and the **Word List**. Write words from the **Word List** on the correct lines inside the squares.

Word List

1. people
2. toys with wheels
3. cherry tomatoes
4. tomatoes
5. my parents
6. fruits and vegetables

A.

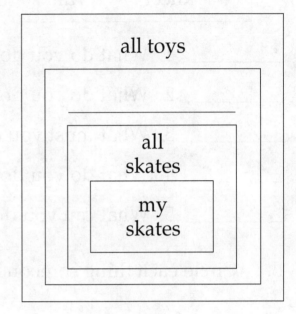

B.

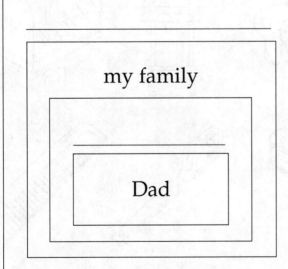

C.

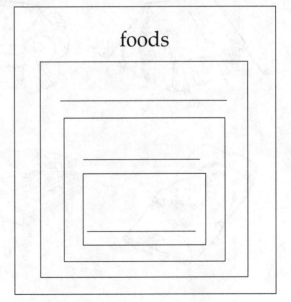

Logic of Actions

A. Read each question. Find the answer in the **Word Box**. Write the word on the line.

Word Box

kneel	run	jump	climb	sit

_____ 1. What do you do when you eat dinner?

_____ 2. What do you do if you want to go faster?

_____ 3. What must you do to paint the bottom of a door?

_____ 4. What do you do to go up?

_____ 5. What can you do with a rope?

B.   Circle each thing someone might take on a camping trip.

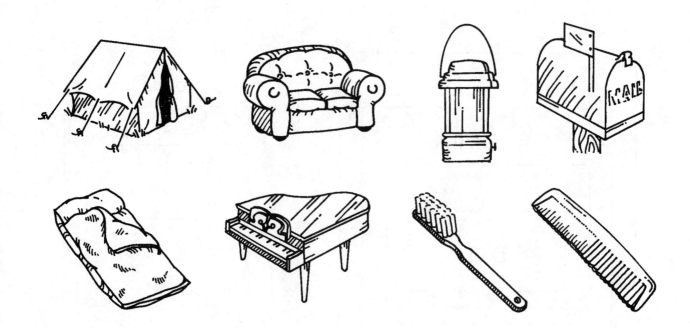

Logic of Actions

Look at the pictures and words under them. Read each sentence. If the boy could use **all three things** to do that job, draw a line under the sentence.

scissors   paint   glue

1. He could help fix a bulletin board.

2. He could fix breakfast.

3. He could decorate his toy box.

4. He could make a picture.

5. He could mow the grass.

6. He could make a get-well card.

7. He could make a storybook.

8. He could fix his wagon.

Critical Thinking 2, SV 6213-X

Logic of Actions

A. Read the list of people's jobs in the box. Write the name of the person who would best solve each problem.

dentist	veterinarian	police officer
plumber	mechanic	doctor

1. You would call a _____ if you had a leaky sink.

2. You would call a _____ if you saw a lost child.

3. You would call a _____ if your dog was sick.

4. You would call a _____ if you weren't feeling well.

5. You would call a _____ if your car wouldn't start.

6. You would call a _____ if you had a tooth that hurt.

B. Finish each sentence by putting an **X** in front of the part that makes sense.

1. Mom's birthday is coming, so Peter should buy a _____.

   _____ present for her   _____ book for himself

2. Maria's best friend is sick, so she should _____.

   _____ send a get-well card   _____ invite her over this afternoon

3. Andres is leaving on a trip tomorrow, so he should _____.

   _____ go roller-skating   _____ start packing a suitcase

                                      Critical Thinking 2, SV 6213-X

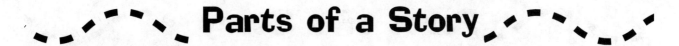

Parts of a Story

Teacher Note

After pupils read the story independently, tell them to circle the first character in the story. Tell them to put Xs on the names of the two people in the story. Tell them to draw a line under the words that tell where the robot was when the story began.

A. A story has characters   WHO?
    A story has a setting   WHERE?
    Read the story. Then follow your teacher's directions.

    The robot was standing in the toy store window. It didn't like it there. It wanted someone to take it home and play with it.
    Rosa walked by the store with her grandpa.
    "Oh, what a wonderful robot!" said Rosa.
    "I will get it for you for your birthday," said Grandpa.
    Grandpa and Rosa went into the store. Grandpa bought the robot. He and Rosa drove it home in the car. The robot enjoyed the ride.
    Rosa played with the robot. Now the robot was happy, and so was Rosa!

B. A story has action.   WHAT HAPPENED?
    Complete each sentence with a word from the story.

    1. Rosa wanted the _____.

    2. Rosa and Grandpa went into the _____.

    3. They took the new toy home in Grandpa's _____.

    4. Rosa played with the _____.

    5. Rosa felt _____.

Parts of a Story

Teacher Note

Tell pupils to: 1) put an X on the names of the people in the story; 2) draw a line under the two sentences that tell where Brian was; 3) circle the sentence that tells what happened to Brian when he didn't get to the corner in time; and 4) put a check by the sentence that tells what Mom will do.

Read the story. Then follow your teacher's directions.

The school bus stopped at the corner. The bus driver looked around. Then the bus went on.

Brian saw the bus. Brian was running along the sidewalk. But he was not at the corner in time. Poor Brian! He missed the bus!

Brian stood at the corner. He had tears in his eyes. What should he do?

Then his mother came along in her car.

"What is wrong, Brian?" she asked.

"I missed the bus," Brian answered.

"Hop in. I'll take you to school," she said.

Story Logic

A. Use the numbers 1-5 to show the story in order. Write the numbers on the lines under the pictures.

_____   _____   _____

_____   _____

B. What three things might the clown do after the show?
Tell the things in order.

1. _____

2. _____

3. _____

Story Logic

Read the words in the **Word Box**. Then read the story. Write a word from the **Word Box** in each blank.

Word Box

path	noise	Jeff	glad
leaves	dark	walking	run
dog	feet	Rags	afraid

One day Jeff went _____ in the woods.

As he walked, he heard the dry _____ under his

_____. He saw many tall trees. It was _____

in the woods. Then _____ saw some big, round eyes.

They looked down at him. Jeff began to _____. He

was _____. A rabbit ran across his _____.

Then he heard another _____. It was his _____,

Rags. Jeff was _____ to see _____!

Critical Thinking 2, SV 6213-X

Recognizing True and False

If you said that something is either **here** or **gone**, you would be right. But, if you said that people have either brown or blue eyes, you would not be right. Some people have green eyes.

Put an **X** before each sentence that is not right because there may be more than two ways it can be.

_____ 1. A dog may be either black or white.

_____ 2. A branch may either have leaves or be bare.

_____ 3. A doctor may be either a man or a woman.

_____ 4. A safety pin may be either open or closed.

_____ 5. A baby may be either a boy or a girl.

_____ 6. Fruit may be either grapes or oranges.

_____ 7. You may go either up or down on a ladder.

_____ 8. Water may be either hot or cold.

Critical Thinking 2, SV 6213-X

Recognizing True and False

Put **X** before each sentence that is probably not all true. Then underline the word that could be changed to make the sentence true.

_____ 1. Roy's parents let all the kids play in their yard.

_____ 2. They can always go swimming.

_____ 3. Some children have pets.

_____ 4. Nine people are going on this trip.

_____ 5. This is the best cereal of all.

_____ 6. All of Mike's clothes are new, so why can't I have some?

_____ 7. We're the only ones that don't have a swimming pool.

_____ 8. There will be a big circus in town soon.

_____ 9. Nobody will be wearing dresses to the party.

_____ 10. Everybody knows that joke.

Critical Thinking 2, SV 6213-X

·Unit 4 Assessment Test

A. Judging Completeness

Three people have forgotten to put on a part of their special suits. Draw the missing things there they belong.

B. Thinking About Facts That Fit

Imagine the captain asks you to come on the flight. Write a question you would ask before saying **yes** or **no**.

_____

_____

C. Logic of Actions

Suzi will be a reporter on the space trip. When she returns, she will tell her classmates about the trip, and show them pictures. Name two things she should take.

_____   _____

Critical Thinking 2, SV 6213-X   **93**

Unit 4 Assessment Test, p. 2

D. **Story Logic**
    Parts of a Story
    Recognizing True and False

Read the poem. Then answer the questions.

The Juice Box Tree

The juice boxes grow on the juice box tree,
Lots of flavors - get 'em for free.
Grape and cherry and orange and lime,
I'll drink plenty when it's time.
I'm watching and waiting all day and night.
They better be ready when it gets light.

1. Has the speaker drunk any juice yet?_____

2. Could juice boxes really grow on a tree?_____

3. For what is the speaker waiting ?_____

E. **Abstract or Concrete**

Write your own poem on a sheet of paper. Tell about something you cannot hold or touch. Use the **Idea Box** to help you get started.

Idea Box

friendship
love   fear
anger

                    Critical Thinking 2, SV 6213-X

Answer Key

Page 6, 7 - A. Serve it with tea., May we have more?; B. I. A. giraffe, B. elephant, II. A. puppy, B. kitten; C. deer-pond, bird-tree, bee-hive; D. 3, 1, 4, 2

Page 9 - 1. c, f; 2. b, e; 3. a, d

Page 10 - 1. sandal, boot; 2. cat, hamster; 3. bus, bicycle; 4. peas, corn; 5. bed, crib

Page 11 - Bedroom: bed, dresser, pillow, blanket, sheet **Bathroom:** tub, shampoo, toothpaste, washcloth, shower **Kitchen:** table, stove, toaster, plate, dishwasher

Page 12 - 1. D, 2. G, 3. H, 4. A, 5. C, 6. B, 7. F, 8. E

Page 13 - 1. bird: A, D; poodle: E, H; jacket: I, J; chair: B, F; top: C, G

2. cat: B, I; flower: A, E; house: F, H; apple: C, G; ring: D, J

Page 14 - Circle 1, 2, 3, 5; X on rowboat with people

Page 15 - 1. M, 2. R, 3. R, 4. M 5. M, 6. M, 7. R, 8. M, 9. M, 10. M, 11. M, 12. M, 13. R, 14. M, 15. R

Page 16 - 1. M, D; 2. M, H; 3. M, B; 4. M, J; 5. R, A; 6. R, F; 7. R, E; 8. R, C; 9. R, I; 10. M, G

Page 17 - Real: My sister tells funny stories. My lizard has four legs. I often drink milk while eating. **Make-believe:** I saw a purple dog. My house is made of peanut butter. A sock gets hungry at lunchtime.

Page 18 - 1. F, 2. F, 3. O, 4. O, 5. F, 6. O, 7. F, 8. O, 9. F, 10. F, 11. O, 12. O, 13. F, 14. O, 15. O

Page 19 - A. 1. D, 2. G, 3. A, 4. B, 5. H, 6. E, 7. C, 8. F; B. Answers will vary.

Page 20 - I think the mystery story booth was the most interesting. I think my poster was the best one. It was the best Book Fair in the whole world!

Page 21 - Answers will vary.

Page 22 - A. 4, 1, 2, 5, 3; B. 3, 4, 2, 1, 5

Page 23 - A. 3, 2, 4, 1; B. 2, 3, 4, 1, 1, 4, 2, 3

Page 24 - 1. hat, 2. bat, 3. pencil, 4. yoyo, 5. banana, 6. dolphin

Page 25 - 1. pencil, pen, crayon; 2. hammer, nail, saw; 3. swan, duck, pelican

Page 26 - Bud: 1. happy face, 2. short, 3. no hair, 4. tiny hat, 5. small coat

Babs: 1. big hat, 2. big pants, 3. tall, 4. sad face, 5. curly hair

Page 27 - 1. stays outside, barks at squirrels, plays with Ted; 2. black kitten, stays in the house, sleeps in a chair, purrs

Page 28 - I. baby duck, A. little, B. fluffy, C. yellow, D. quack

II. turtle, A. tiny, B. shell, C. body, D. inside the shell

Page 29 - I. A. made of sun-dried earth called adobe, B. roof of one was floor of another

II. A. made of logs covered with earth, B. dome-shaped roofs

Page 30-31 - A. Circle elephant, monkey, lion, horse; X on rabbit, kitten, dog

B. I. A. giraffe, B. elephant

II. A. puppy, B. kitten

C. fact, make-believe, opinion

Page 32 - 1. D, 2. B, 3. D, 4. C, 5. A, 6. D

Page 33 - 1. They are all people. 2. You can live in them. 3. They are plants. 4. They are young animals. 5. They all have wheels. 6. They are used for writing. 7. They are used for sewing.

Page 34 - birds, little, short, two, beak

Page 35 - C. paint, wallpaper, carpet, tile

Page 36 - A. 2. low, 3. pay, 4. pin

B. 2. our, 3. barn, 4. bell

Page 37 - 3, 4, 1, 2

Page 38 - 3, 1, 4, 5, 2

Page 39 - A. 1, 2, 3; B. 1, 3, 2; C. 3, 1, 2; D. 3, 2, 1 E. 3, 2, 1

Page 40 - A. 1. Tina got the things to build a fort. 2. Tina built the fort. 3. Tina made a sign and put it up.

B. 1. The kitten got stuck in a tree. 2. Uncle Carlos brought a ladder. 3. He rescued the kitten.

Page 41 Make sure students colored correctly.

Page 42 - E, F, H, I, K, L, M, N, T, V, W, X, Y, Z

Page 43 - A. 1. bold, afraid; 2. same, different; 3. nice, bad

B. 1. small, big; 2. shining, dull; 3. smash, mend

C. 1. tall, short; 2. fast, slow; 3. ill, well

Page 44 - 1. to, 2. two, 3. rode, 4. road, 5. flower, 6. flour, 7 be, 8. bee, 9. would, 10. wood

Page 45 - A. 1, B. 2, C. 3

Page 46 - 1. Cactus is a desert plant. 2. Oranges change color. 3. Carrots are root vegetables. 4. Cotton needs warm weather.

Page 47 - 1. Jackie was getting ready for a costume party. 2. The parade was so much fun! 3. A sunrise is very beautiful. 4. Mark wanted to paint a picture.

Page 48 - 1. Here is how to make a (mask.) 2. (Skyrockets) are beautiful. 3. (Tadpoles) are young frogs. 4. Ben got a (surprise) for his birthday. 5. Nancy was going to give her dog a (bath.) 6. The (sun) is important to everthing on Earth.

Page 49 - 3, 5, 1, 6, 4, 2

Page 50 - police officer: hat, badge; **firefighter:** hat, hose; **chef:** hat, pot; **carpenter:** saw, hammer; **astronaut:** helmet, spacesuit; **nurse:** stethoscope, thermometer

Page 51 - 1. C, 2. B, 3. D, 4. A, 5. E, F, 6. G, H

Page 52 - 1. won, 2. nail, 3. out, 4. pencil, 5. party, 6. Tuesday, 7. red, 8. water, 9. baseball, bat, 10. hungry, apple

Page 53-54 - A. deer - water, bird - tree, bee - hive

B. 3, 1, 4, 2 Possible title: How to Build a Doghouse

C. 1. ox, 2. rat, 3. ape, 4. eel, 5. pig, 6. ant, tern

Page 55 - A. 3, 2, 4, 1

B. 2, 3, 1, 4

C. 2, 1, 4, 3

D. 2, 3, 1, 4

Page 56 - 1. square, 2. \\ , 3. X, 4. S, 5. add last petal of flower, 6. PxE, 7. 7, 8. upside down and backwards L-shaped box, 9. two parallel upright rectangles

Page 57 - A. Drawing should show three balloons. B. Drawing should show two birds hatched, one egg still unhatched. C. Drawing should show one mitten and one boot *or* two boots.

Page 58 - x on last box, crayon box

Page 59 - 1. 3, 2. 2, 3. 1, 4. 1, 5. 3, 6. 1, 7.3

Page 60 - 1. Tom's house, 2. Mark's house, 3. the park, 4. Sue's house, 5. Lee

Page 61 - 1. 30 seconds, 2. 30 minutes, 3. 2 years, 4. 2 minutes, 5. 15 minutes, 6. 4 minutes

Page 62 - A. 2, B. 1, C. 3, D. 2

Page 63 - 1. grow, 2. read it, 3. have fun, 4. go on a trip, 5. cold, 6. sad, 7. good, 8. read it

Page 64 - Sentences will vary.

Page 65 - Responses will vary.

Page 66 - 1. no, 2. no, 3. yes, 4. no, 5. no, 6. yes

Page 67 - A. Circle glass of water, X 2

B. Circle key, X 3

Page 68 - A. circle the mail carrier, X 3

B. circle a kangaroo, X 3

Page 69 - 1. dime, 2. work, 3. picked, 4. pizza, 5. play

Page 70 - A. 1, B. 4, C. 5, D. 3, E. 2, F. 6

Page 71 - A, B, B, A, A, B

Page 72 - 1. borrowed, 2. help, 3. give. 4. watch, 5. left, 6. finished, 7. come

Page 73 - bill - A, pet - A, left - B,

pen - B, line - B

line, pen, bill, pet, left

Page 74-75 - A. 1. 2, 4, 5, 1, 6, 3; 2. Princess, It is larger than Zip.; 3. Flipper, It is lighter. (or) It is made for just one person.

B. Serve it with tea,

May we have more?

C. Answers will vary.

Page 76 - Look at pictures to determine completeness.

Page 77 - 1. picture, 2. wheel, 3. short, 4. handle, 5. door, 6. hands

Page 78 - 1. A little clown rode a huge bicycle.

2. Three strong acrobats made a pyramid.

3. A magician pulled an umbrella from a top hat.

4. A woman walked on a wire in the air.

5. A juggler threw rings high into the air.

Page 79 - 1. 1 and 2, 2. 1 and 3, 3. 2 and 3, 4. 1 and 2

Page 80 - 1, 3, 6, 8

Page 81 - 1. pretty, silly, mean, idea, angry, lazy, happy, funny, busy

2. scarf, ball, egg, pen, flower, button, fish, crayon, bicycle, kitten, pencil

Page 82 - 1. oak trees; 2. furniture, my rocking chair

Page 83 - A. toys with wheels; B. people, my parents; C. fruits and vegetables, tomatoes, cherry tomatoes

Page 84 - A. 1. sit, 2. run, 3. kneel, 4. climb, 5. jump

B. tent, lantern, sleeping bag, toothbrush, comb

Page 85 - 1, 3, 4, 6, 7

Page 86 - A. 1. plumber, 2. police officer, 3. veterinarian, 4. doctor, 5. mechanic, 6. dentist

B. 1. present for her, 2. send a get well card, 3. start packing a suitcase

Page 87 - A. Circle robot, X Rose, grandpa; Underline in the toy store window

B. 1. robot, 2. store, 3. car, 4. robot, 5. happy

Page 88 - X bus driver, Brian, mother

Underline Brian was running along the sidewalk. Brian stood on the corner.

Circle He missed the bus!

Check "Hop in. I'll take you to school." she said.

Page 89 - A. 3, 4 or 5, 1, 4 or 5, 2

B. Answers will vary.

Page 90 - walking, leaves, feet, dark, Jeff, run, afraid, path, noise, dog, glad, Rags

Page 91 - 1, 6, 8

Page 92 - 1. all, 2. always, 5. best, 6. All, 7. only, 9. Nobody, 10. Everybody

Page 93-94 - A. Answers will vary.

B. Answers will vary.

C. Answers will vary.

D. 1. no, 2. no, 3. He or she is waiting for the juice boxes to be ready to pick.

E. Answers will vary.

Critical Thinking 2, SV 6213-X